FAMOUS AVIATORS OF WORLD WAR II

JAMES B. SWEENEY

Lieutenant Colonel,
U.S. Air Force (Retired)

Famous Aviators OF World War II

Franklin Watts
New York | London | Toronto | Sydney | 1987
A First Book

Photographs courtesy of:
Smithsonian Institution: pp. 19, 31, 44, 56;
U.S. Air Force: pp. 20, 33, 34, 46, 52, 62, 71, 72, 76;
Photo Archives, The Ohio State University: p. 41;
The Collections of the Library of Congress: p. 68

Library of Congress Cataloging-in-Publication Data

Sweeney, James B.
Famous aviators of World War II.

(A First book)
Bibliography: p.
Includes index.
Summary: Presents biographical sketches of five
American fighter pilots and aviation heroes of World
War II. Includes description of the types of aircraft,
a glossary of aviation terms, and explanations of
military ranks and command structure in the U.S. Air
Force.
1. World War, 1939–1945—Aerial operations, American
—Juvenile literature. 2. Air pilots, Military—United
States—Biography—Juvenile literature. 3. Generals—
United States—Biography—Juvenile literature.
4. United States. Army Air Forces—Biography—Juvenile
literature. [1. Air pilots, Military. 2. United
States. Army Air Forces—Biography. 3. World War,
1939–1945—Aerial operations, American] I. Title.
D790.S969 1987   940.54'4973'0922 [B]   86-23339
ISBN 0-531-10302-1

This book is
respectfully
dedicated to

John R. Dennis
Harry Edward Neal
Geraldine Kelly

CONTENTS

Introduction
10

Claire L. Chennault
12

James H. Doolittle
22

Curtis E. LeMay
36

Emmett O'Donnell, Jr.
48

Carl Spaatz
64

Officer Rank
During World War II
79

U.S. Air Force
Command Structure
During
World War II
81

Glossary
of World War II
Aviation Terms
83

Types of
Aircraft
87

Bibliography
89

Index
91

With sincere thanks to Dave Barr,
Ed Alcott, Mike Martinez, Ruth Murphy,
residents of Air Force Village, Texas,
and members of the Officer Training
School Library (Medina AFB), Texas.

INTRODUCTION

It takes many men and women to defend a great nation in time of national conflict. World War II proved this when Pearl Harbor was attacked on December 7, 1941. It was then that America's armed forces grew from a mere handful of people to over nine million citizens under arms. Throughout this gigantic military expansion, various degrees of leadership were demonstrated from privates to generals. Regardless of rank, every man and woman possessed a quality common to all—they were Americans.

As young people, each of these military leaders had labored through a required amount of schooling, was possessed of dreams, experienced failures, tasted success, and recognized the need for further education.

All seemed to sense that life was a struggle. The harder a person fought—with whatever means were available—the higher up the ladder he was able to climb.

To prove this assertion, five great aviators have been selected out of the thousands of men who served in the U.S. Army Air Corps. None had an exclusive on leadership. Each had to thrust himself forward and prove that his knowledge, his imagination, his beliefs were better than those of any other man or woman.

Yet none of these five was born with a halo around his head. All were average students: good in some subjects, poor in others. But whatever their strengths and weaknesses, they never ceased to enhance the one and overcome the other. They worked with what they had. They made do. They fashioned their own version of success out of what was at hand.

World War II developed numerous other great aviators, hundreds upon hundreds of them. Any man who ever risked flying over enemy territory was indeed a hero. No single volume is large enough to contain all such names. These five are merely representative of the others who lived through the horrors of war in order to preserve the freedoms we now enjoy.

It has been my rare good fortune to have met and talked with all five of the aviators mentioned.

Place of birth: Commerce, Texas.

Date of birth: September 6, 1890.

Date of death: July 27, 1958.

Education: Louisiana State Normal School, graduated 1911. Numerous military schools.

Married: First marriage to Nell Thompson. Second marriage to Anna Chan, December 21, 1947.

Characteristics: A born fighter (both physically and mentally), determined, ambitious, a perceptive planner. Nicknamed Radical Chennault because of his innovative thinking.

Major commands and accomplishments:

1917 commissioned first lieutenant following graduation from Officer's Training School to serve in World War I.

1920 commissioned first lieutenant, Air Service, Regular Army.

1923 named commander of the Nineteenth Pursuit Squadron.

1937 retired with rank of major.

1941 designated brigadier general in the Chinese Air Force and formed the "Flying Tigers."

1942 recalled by U.S. Air Corps and placed on duty as a colonel; promoted to brigadier general.

1943 promoted to major general.

1958 promoted to lieutenant general.

CLAIRE L. CHENNAULT

Life was a struggle. The Chennault boy found this out at an early age after his mother died. The family of four boys—William, Nelson, Joe, and Claire—moved from Texas to Louisiana where Mr. Chennault became manager of a cotton plantation.

That move left Claire in a world of busy grown-ups who had little time to spend with an energetic, curious youngster. He had to make do with whatever was at hand.

Luckily, there was "Uncle Joe" nearby. Uncle Joe was a black plantation worker who enjoyed a status of semiretirement. Old Uncle Joe didn't know much about what came out of books, but he knew how to tree a possum, bait a trout line, and put a pack of hounds on the trail of a mountain lion. He was also a very good rough-and-tumble fighter who understood how to shoot a gun so that you hit whatever was in your sights. Best of all, Uncle Joe had a flair for teaching.

Uncle Joe taught young Chennault whatever was necessary to survive in a world of swamps, poisonous snakes, and animals that fought back if you missed with your first shot. This was Louisiana plantation living.

But there was a price for Uncle Joe's teaching. Claire Chennault had to help the old man with the chores, and there was plenty of work to be done. Young Claire had to help draw water out of the well (almost a full-time job for a plantation housing barnyard animals and thirsty humans), slop the pigs, cut firewood, milk the cows, and gather eggs from the chicken coop. He had a bed to make, a room to keep neat, and indoor pets to be cared for. His was a busy life.

Then there was school.

Claire didn't take kindly to that. He preferred the sort of teaching Uncle Joe did: subjects like survival; how to fight back if a stranger tried to rough things up. Muscle, that's what counted—good physical conditioning. Claire worked at keeping his body in tip-top form. He enjoyed the outdoors and found a challenge in pitting himself against the rigors of nature.

But with maturity came the realization that there was something missing. While his body was strong, his mind was being neglected. A youngster of great imagination, given to daydreaming in school, Claire turned to books worthy of his attention. He read volumes like *The Adventures of Tom Sawyer, Treasure Island, Ivanhoe, Ben Hur*, and other books that offered exciting reading. He devoured adventure, for he envied great warriors such as Julius Caesar, Napoleon, and George Washington. They had what he wanted most—leadership.

At eighteen, Claire was fully grown. He was five feet ten, lean, tough-muscled, and dark-eyed, with deep brown hair. His skin showed the ruddiness of an outdoorsman. The family disputed the young man's future education. His father thought his rugged son's future lay in farming. One uncle was a schoolteacher and felt Claire should go to a school that trained students to be teachers. Another relative maintained that the youth would make a fine soldier.

In an attempt to decide his own future, Claire applied to both West Point and Annapolis. When the Navy came through, he left for Annapolis to take the entrance exams. Upon arrival, he looked the academy over and decided the buildings were too confining for a country boy like himself. He turned around and went home.

Claire's father then insisted that he attend Louisiana State University as a student-cadet. Claire did so and was assigned to room six in building B of what had become known as "The Old War Skule." At that time, hazing was still in vogue. Older students found pleasure in harassing freshmen with abusive and humiliating tricks. Claire Chennault, the unsophisticated country boy, seemed like a prime prospect for a few laughs. In order to accomplish this, a group of upper-class cadets gave him a sabre and issued strict orders that he was to stand at attention, let no one enter or leave the dormitory building, and remain on post until relieved by the officer of the day.

"Are those orders clear?" one of the senior cadets demanded.

"They are, sir," Chennault replied. "I will remain on duty until relieved by the officer of the day, and above all, I will let no one enter or leave this building."

"Excellent," the group leader replied, and with that they entered the building. Going to an open window directly above the hapless Chennault, they dumped a bucket of water onto his head. Chennault never stirred. The upperclassmen were disappointed, so they tried a second bucket of water. It was right on target, yet Claire Chennault refused to move. A third and fourth bucket of water produced no better results. The senior cadets tired of such a pointless game. They busied themselves with other matters.

"Ah," a hungry upperclassman said, "there goes chow call. Let's go, men."

All raced for the one exit out of the building. There they were met by a sabre-armed freshman with orders that no one was to leave the building until he was relieved by the officer of the day. The upperclassmen pleaded and cajoled, all to no effect. Their joke had backfired, and young Chennault was making sure that it hurt them more than it had hurt him.

After a lapse of time, and the loss of everyone's dinner, the officer of the day was called and the freshman properly relieved of his post. After that, young Mr. Chennault was no longer subject to hazing. His standing in the student body was further enhanced when he was talked into a boxing match with a Navy middleweight fighter. Claire went the full ten-round limit. He didn't win the match, but he gave as good as he took. It wasn't until the conclusion of the fight that he learned his opponent was the All-Navy Middleweight Champion. That infuriated him. In typical Chennault fashion, he challenged the Navy man to a rough-and-tumble match. The Navy boxer declined the invitation.

As a college student, it became increasingly difficult for Claire Chennault to both study and earn tuition money. Personal finances became tight. While at home one summer, his relative who was a schoolteacher dropped by the house. He advised Claire to become a teacher as there were jobs to be had. Claire did so, graduating from Louisiana State Normal School as a qualified teacher.

Claire Chennault was given a teaching job in a tough community. The students prided themselves on how difficult they were to handle. The first day on the job was a bit disorderly. However, after Claire had roughed up a couple of the biggest students into submission, there was no further trouble. From then on, Chennault emphasized sports. Baseball was his favorite team recreation, and in time the school produced a state champion baseball team. Chennault stayed at the institution for four more years, leaving the school as principal.

It was then that fate directed Claire Chennault into the field of aviation. World War I had been in progress for several years when the United States was forced to join with England in helping defeat the German Kaiser. Chennault abandoned his promising future in education and volunteered for military service. Because of his college degree, he was sent to Officer's Training School, Fort Benjamin Harris, Indiana. After completing a course of studies, he was commissioned a first lieutenant in the infantry reserves. By November 1917, he had managed to transfer to the Aviation Section, Signal Reserve Corps.

On April 9, 1920, Claire Chennault resigned his temporary wartime commission and accepted a permanent commission in the peacetime army. In that capacity, he served at numerous air bases around the continental United States. During 1923 he was stationed at the Hawaiian Department. While on this tour of duty, he became commander of the Nineteenth Pursuit Squadron.

As commander of the Nineteenth, Chennault was able to use his imagination. He developed new flying procedures and attack capabilities. He is also credited with developing a technique of parachuting heavy artillery weapons to ground forces. He was rated by his superior officers an outstanding authority on pursuit flying, a fearless aviator, and a competent leader. Upon reassignment to the continental United States, he organized a team of stunt flyers into what became known as "Three Men on a Flying Trapeze." The trio performed at many public gatherings, such as the Cleveland Air Races of both 1934 and 1935.

Promotions in the military were slow. The outlook was not encouraging. Chennault, despite his innovative work in aviation, remained a first lieutenant from 1920 until 1929, at which time he was made a captain. Finally, in 1936, he attained the rank of major. By then, he and his first wife Nell had eight children. Since he had become hard of hearing from too many hours of flying in open-cockpit planes, he chose to retire. He settled his family in a cottage bordering Lake St. John, close to the town of Waterproof, Louisiana.

Retirement was not for Claire Chennault. He was too energetic, too ambitious, too imaginative. One of his flying buddies offered him a job with the Chinese Air Force. He snapped it up. By July 1937, he was in China. That's when he discovered how difficult a job he'd agreed to undertake. The Japanese were invading China, and a General Chiang Kai-shek was trying to strike back with an air force of fewer than one hundred planes.

Chennault's fighting spirit surfaced. With odds of a thousand to one against him, he reorganized Chinese air power into a strike force. His years of teaching paid off. Slowly, patiently, he introduced new flying tactics. Playing on Japanese superstitions, Claire Chennault had the Chinese paint each P-40 plane to resemble a huge shark. The planes were called Flying Tiger Sharks. This was later shortened to two words that caused great fear in the hearts of Japanese fighter pilots—Flying Tigers!

Chennault needed experienced fighter pilots. To meet his needs, he turned to venturesome Americans. He offered aviators six hundred dollars a month salary, plus five hundred dollars for every Japanese plane they shot down. During those days, such an amount was fabulous. Many young men leaped at the opportunity. It was then Chennault formed the American Volunteer Group (AVG) and whipped the organization into a team of combat pilots.

"Japan," Chennault wrote to many congressmen in Washington, D.C., "will someday strike at America from the air."

Unfortunately, no one in the United States Congress believed that such an event could take place. Receiving very little aid from the United States, the Flying Tigers fought the Japanese air force with what few planes they possessed. Their kill ratio was amazing. The AVG knocked out thirty-two Japanese pilots for every Flying Tiger lost. This was a record never before or since surpassed.

It was a tough struggle for Chennault and his Flying Tigers. They had only a few combat-weary planes, a small supply of gasoline, no replacement parts, and a dwindling number of trained pilots. Nevertheless, they still had an ace in the hole—Claire Chennault. He knew fighter tactics and could foresee upcoming Japanese treachery.

Chiang Kai-shek promoted Claire Chennault to the rank of brigadier general in the Chinese Air Force. This was during the summer of 1941. It was about this time that America became concerned over the growing military might of the Japanese. Suddenly convinced that America did in fact stand in danger, the U.S. Army

Brigadier General Chennault (second from left) plans strategy with some of his flyers.

recalled Claire Chennault to active duty. He was promoted to colonel in the United States Army Air Corps.

Although Chennault was promoted to brigadier general after only five days as a colonel, he was not happy over the end of the American Volunteer Group (AVG). Only a few of his pilots followed him into the U.S. Army Air Corps, while most of the mechanics went their own way. Nevertheless, Chennault took command of the United States air forces in China.

Claire Chennault advocated strengthening air power at the expense of ground forces. This put him at odds with higher ranking Army officers. Most of these senior officers were from the ground forces and firm believers in infantrymen. Chennault's argument was that the Chinese Army was a shambles and not to be relied upon. Nevertheless, the man from Louisiana gave the job all he could muster. On March 22, 1943, he was promoted to major general and awarded his second star.

On August 14, 1945, Japan surrendered to Allied forces and withdrew from China. That put an end to World War II. Chennault resigned his command on July 6, 1945. On December 21, 1947, in Hungjao, Shanghai, China, General Chennault, having divorced his first wife, married Anna Chan of Peking. Subsequently, they had two children. Although he was no longer on active duty, the U.S. Army Air Corps saw fit to award him his third star. On July 25, 1958, he was promoted to the rank of lieutenant general.

On July 27, 1958, Claire Chennault died.

It was the end of a great warrior, but not the end of his public acclaim. On November 14, 1958, Lake Charles Air Force Base, in Louisiana, was renamed Chennault Air Force Base, a permanent tribute to one of this nation's most famous World War II aviators.

Capt. Claire Chennault

Place of birth: Alameda, California.

Date of birth: December 14, 1896.

Education: University of California–1917. Massachusetts Institute of Technology, 1923–1925.

Marriage: Josephine Daniels.

Nickname: Jimmy.

Characteristics: Aggressive, physically active, loved boxing, combative, hot-tempered, inclined to perform in an unexpected—and sometimes foolhardy—manner.

Major commands and accomplishments:

1918 commissioned a second lieutenant in Aviation Section, Signal Reserve Corps.

1920 commissioned a first lieutenant in Regular Army. As a lieutenant colonel, U.S. Army Reserve, commanded the "First Special Aviation Project."

1942 lead air attack on Japan from aircraft carrier U.S.S. *Hornet*; received Congressional Medal of Honor and promoted to brigadier general.

1943 became commanding general of Fifteenth Air Force.

1944 took command of the Eighth Air Force and promoted to lieutenant general.

1946 became director of Shell Oil Company.

1959 board chairman, Space Technology Laboratory.

1961 director of Mutual of Omaha Insurance Company.

1985 promoted to four-star general by President Reagan.

JAMES H. DOOLITTLE

He was the sort of youngster a bully enjoys picking on: small, with curly hair that his mother liked to let grow long, and dimpled cheeks. The impression that Jimmy Doolittle conveyed was that of a delicate, spoiled brat. In Nome, Alaska, during the gold rush era, such a physical appearance was like asking every browbeater in school to take a poke at you. The boy didn't look like the type who would hit back. In fact, he wasn't. So the older boys enjoyed taking a crack at him.

This is what started Jimmy Doolittle taking stock of both his surroundings and himself. He was tired of being the butt of every nasty trick going around the school. The frontier town of Nome was a rough place. The population consisted of hunters, Eskimo fishermen, gamblers, hard-rock miners, and Indian trappers, plus any wives daring enough to come along with their children.

Throughout most of the summer, streets were knee-deep in mud. During winter the mud froze into ruts as solid as iron. Buildings consisted of winterized tents or wooden shacks. They housed saloons, gun shops, dance halls, and a one-room schoolhouse that was without indoor toilets and possessed only a potbellied stove for heat.

Nome, in the late 1800s, had neither church nor jail. It was a town without spiritual or physical guidance. Drinking was big business and criminal claim-jumping a way of life. Transportation was by boat during the summer and dogsled in the winter. Only the sturdy were destined to survive, and Jimmy Doolittle wasn't very rugged. Or so the roughnecks attending classes in the unfriendly schoolhouse seemed to think.

Jimmy Doolittle decided otherwise. He had certain characteristics going for himself. He was quick on his feet and had a temper that gave him drive, but which he learned to control. He decided to combine these assets and try them out on the next bully giving him a hard time.

Jimmy didn't have long to wait. One day a brawny lad began to shove him around. That did it. The harmless little Jimmy clenched his fists and leaped at his adversary. A series of quick, hard punches dropped the bruiser to the ground. Onlookers had to drag the Doolittle kid away from the fray and keep him pinned down until his temper cooled.

Word spread quickly that the cute kid with the curls was a hellion with his fists. This caused two reactions. Some youngsters avoided Jimmy because he was too explosive to pal around with. Several of the more burly lads, however, decided to test his skills. As a consequence, Jimmy did a lot of fighting with few or no backers. Eventually, his tormentors accepted the fact that the kid with the dimples was a good fighter. In truth, it was Jimmy Doolittle's determination that carried him to victory. Once tormented into anger, nothing seemed able to stop the lightninglike strike of his fists.

Even the neighbors began to sit up and take notice. Questions were asked. Who were these Doolittles and where did they come from? Why were they here? Frank Doolittle, Jimmy's father, was an itinerant carpenter. His mother was a lovely lady named Rosa. They had come to Nome from Alameda, California, where their son had been born, because Frank Doolittle was a dreamer and a drifter. He had visions of hitting it rich in the goldfields, but he had to revert to carpentry so that his family could have food on the table.

Jimmy, their only child, had been born on December 14, 1896. Six months later his father joined the gold rush and took off for Alaska. His wife and child followed in 1900, arriving after a stormy sea voyage of close to 2,500 miles (4,000 km). Both were put to work upon arrival. Rosa did the washing, cooking, ironing, and other household chores. Jimmy was charged with keeping the woodbox filled, supplying water for the household, and fighting his way through the lower grades at school. As it turned out, he was better at fighting than at studies.

Eventually, Rosa decided that there was no future for her son in Alaska. She wanted Jimmy to be exposed to a little culture, not the constant rowdiness of Alaska. In 1908, after the spring thaw had broken up the ice, she trimmed off Jimmy's curls and announced they were returning to California.

Jimmy hated having to leave his friends and the only environment he could remember behind. With tears in his eyes and sadness in his heart, he watched as the ship pulled away from the dock. He was being taken away from vivid—if brutal—memories. He could recall the horror of seeing a pack of half-wolf sled dogs turn on their master and kill him. Then there was the first public hanging he witnessed: a prospector had murdered three of his partners for a bit of gold. The townsfolk took him out and strung him up to a telephone pole.

Some remembrances were more pleasant. There was the first day he took his own rifle out hunting and shot an elk; the time his Eskimo buddy, Kiyutelluk, taught him how to handle a kayak; the time he saved a baby moose from being attacked by a bear. These were beautiful memories and he'd never forget them. But destiny had earmarked Jimmy Doolittle. There were greater things in store for him than fishing, hunting, and brawling.

Jimmy was not enthusiastic about school. Nevertheless, he entered high school in Los Angeles. His marks indicated that he was barely making a passing grade. Certainly none of his studies

[25]

showed any of the mental brilliance for which he would someday become known. However, he did enjoy—and have a flair for—what was then called shop. It was a course that involved wood-working and the use of machinery and the gasoline engine. It was also in high school that Jimmy learned to box, rather than brawl. A teacher named Forest Bailey showed him how to perform with boxing gloves. Jimmy enjoyed this. At 105 pounds (48 kg), he began to make a name for himself in the field of athletics.

During this time, Jimmy started to become interested in a pretty girl named Josephine—Jo—Daniels. Unfortunately, she had no interest in knockouts, or the results of a ten-round boxing match. Despite this, Jimmy kept on boxing. In 1912, he was named Pacific Coast Bantamweight Amateur Champion. Neither his mother nor Jo Daniels was impressed.

Out in the world, great developments were taking place in the flying of heavier-than-air machines. Headlines were made by a young man named Cromwell Dixon. He built and flew his own aircraft, thus becoming the world's youngest aviator. He was the envy of every American boy, including Jimmy Doolittle. And it didn't take Jo Daniels long to point out that young Dixon was doing better than young Doolittle.

Jimmy entered a junior college. After two years, he switched to an enginering course at the University of California. At that point, he seemed to develop an interest in schoolwork. He also managed to keep up with his athletics. Even though he'd dropped a little in weight, at nineteen years of age he was known as a proficient boxer. He took on many a heavier adversary. It was acknowledged that Jimmy had speed and guts.

While he was in college, war erupted in Europe. It was triggered by the assassination of Archduke Ferdinand of Austria in June 1914. The war kept getting worse until Congress declared that the United States should join with the European Allies. That was in April 1917. Excitement was intense. Many students dropped out of school to join the armed forces. Jimmy was no exception.

Although Jimmy Doolittle had never thought much about aviation up to this point, it now seemed to be the most glamorous branch of the services. He enlisted as a cadet in the Signal Reserve Corps, Aviation Section. When Jo Daniels saw Jimmy in uniform, she was impressed. It was the culminating factor in a long love affair. The two eloped while he was on leave. They were married in the Los Angeles city hall, with Josephine paying for the marriage license. Between them, they had a financial worth of slightly less than twenty dollars. This didn't appear to be much of a foundation on which to build a marriage that was destined to last a lifetime.

In January 1918, Jimmy, the cadet, reported to Rockwell Field, California, and began his training in a Curtiss JN-4. This was the famous "Jenny" of World War I. Later, Doolittle was to admit that it was on his first solo flight that—despite witnessing a fatal accident en route—he fell in love with aviation. From that point on, he was hooked on flying.

March 11, 1918, was the day Doolittle was commissioned a second lieutenant in the Aviation Section, Signal Reserve Corps. One instructor voiced the opinion that ". . . the shrimp has a feel for an airborne plane."

Instead of being given orders to proceed to France and the combat he yearned for, he was assigned to a dry hole in Texas called Camp Dix. Although he did some flying and considerable boxing, it was tiresome duty. He was then twenty-one years old and itching for action.

The only action that came his way while stationed at Camp Dix was an opportunity to fly an incredible machine called a Thomas Morse. It had only two speeds, off and on. It had no throttle and no brakes. To fly the plane you simply flipped the switch on. To land, you twisted the same switch off. After that you were supposed to glide to a safe landing. Without brakes, pilots often found themselves taxiing or gliding into all types of immovable objects.

Later, Jimmy Doolittle was transferred back to Rockwell Field, in California, and selected to be an instructor. He proved to be exceptionally good at this. Unfortunately, to relieve the tedium, Jimmy was given to performing all sorts of flying acrobatics. He was reprimanded on a number of occasions and finally grounded for a month.

Although Jimmy Doolittle's stunt flying never ceased, World War I did. It ended on November 11, 1918, with Jimmy still at Rockwell Field turning out fighter pilots.

Peacetime years hung heavily on the ambitious Jimmy. Promotions were almost nonexistent. As a consequence, it was not until 1920, when he was transferred to Kelly Field, Texas, to attend Air Service Mechanics School, that he received his commission as a first lieutenant in the Regular Army. Even as this was taking place, the size of the military air arm was being reduced. At the height of World War I, there were 195,000 men in the air forces, with 740 airplanes and 77 balloons. Abruptly, this force was reduced to 896 officers and less than 7,500 enlisted men. What few planes remained were leftovers from combat. This presented a grim outlook for an eager young aviator.

But Jimmy Doolittle saw things differently. He perceived the downswing of military life as an opportunity to demonstrate the speed and capabilities of the flying machine. He set about furthering his formal education and racing airplanes. In 1922, Doolittle flew the first continental crossing in less than twenty-four hours. Between October 1923 and June 1925, he attended advanced courses at the Massachusetts Institute of Technology (MIT) in Boston. A few of the subjects he studied were theoretical aeronautics, advanced calculus, and advanced wing theory. Also in 1925, he won the enviable Schneider Trophy Race for seaplanes. During 1927, he became the first man to complete an outside plane loop and live to talk about it. The year 1929 saw him make man's first "blind flight"—through the use of instruments alone. Two years later he won the famed Bendix Trophy, as part of the National Air Races, and in so doing set a new transcontinental speed record between California and Ohio. After setting this record, he immediately refueled and flew to Newark, New Jersey, setting a new coast-to-coast record as the first person to fly across the North American continent in less than twenty-four hours. In 1932, he won the Thompson Trophy Race, a triangular course with three pylons each, 10 miles (16 km) apart, and set a new speed record for landplanes.

While little publicity was given to military flying, the public was aware of both Jimmy Doolittle and his masterful achievements in aviation. Fate, though, was conserving this man's greatest capabilities for more meaningful accomplishments.

During 1933, a power-hungry man named Adolf Hitler became the chancellor of Germany. In 1936, the German army occupied the Rhineland, which province the Germans had lost to the Allies during World War I. In 1939, Britain, France, Australia, and New Zealand declared war on Germany. On December 7, 1941, Japan attacked Pearl Harbor and the United States was again at war.

Jimmy Doolittle, who had returned to civilian life and was accomplishing big things, was recalled to military service. His first step was to convince leaders of the American automobile industry that they should convert their plants to the production of aircraft. Next, he conducted an aviation fact-finding mission to Great Britain. Following that, as a lieutenant colonel, U.S. Army Reserve, he was called upon to command an operation with the cover name "First Special Aviation Project." This was to be the initial bombing of Japan.

American morale needed a shot in the arm. The attack on Pearl Harbor had devastated United States military strength in the Pacific. Citizens were angry, but frustrated. Something big was needed to unify national strength. Jimmy Doolittle gave the country that much-needed boost.

Doolittle organized a force of sixteen B-25 twin-engine, land-based bombers to lift off the deck of an aircraft carrier sailing in the Pacific Ocean. To undertake such a wild scheme called for the heavy planes to be stripped of all excess weight. Radios were removed, most armament was reduced, and guns were kept to a minimum. However, extra fuel tanks had to be added. The net payload, or that part of the cargo which is deliverable, was increased. Volunteer crews were carefully selected and assembled for training at Eglin Field, Florida.

It was on April 2, 1942, that the aircraft carrier U.S.S. *Hornet* left San Francisco with Doolittle's planes aboard and eighty men to crew them. Bad weather beset the carrier. Rough seas dogged their course. Several vital members of the proposed flight became seasick. To make matters even worse, a Japanese patrol boat spotted the carrier. The patrol boat was sunk by gunfire, but not before it could radio a warning message to Tokyo. Because of these regrettable events, Doolittle deemed it wise to lead his bombers into the attack earlier than programmed. He took off in the first bomber to leave the carrier. Five flights of three planes each followed. A total of sixteen bombers headed for Japan.

Despite the brief warning message flashed by the Japanese patrol boat, Doolittle's planes apparently caught Japanese military forces unprepared. His planes dropped bombs on Tokyo, Yokohama, Yokosuka, Kobe, and Nagoya. These successful raids gave American morale a boost and caused the Japanese military to revise their war plans. When President Roosevelt was asked by the press where the planes had come from, he said, Shangri-la. (This was a mythical Tibetan city that was featured in a novel written by James Hilton and at that time was a best seller in America. The Japanese, however, had not heard of the book, and this threw them into a flurry as they sought to find a base called Shangri-la.)

Of the sixteen planes that took off from the deck of the aircraft carrier U.S.S. *Hornet*, all were initially lost. Of the eighty crewmen, one member was drowned when the plane had to be ditched, three were caught and executed by the Japanese, one died in prison, while four survived forty months solitary confinement and were released after the war. One B-25, that piloted by Capt. Edward J. York, landed in Russia, where the plane was con-

*General Spaatz (center) and, to his left, General Jimmy Doolittle,
shown inspecting an experimental device on a United States plane*

fiscated and the crew placed under house arrest. The remainder eventually found their way into friendly hands.

Jimmy Doolittle was immediately awarded this nation's highest miltary decoration, the Congressional Medal of Honor, and promoted to brigadier general. For a while, he was sent hither and yon to give speeches, attend war bond rallies, and stir up national patriotism. But he soon grew tired of the luncheon circuit and asked to be assigned to something more combative. As a result, he was placed in command of the Fourth Bombardment Wing, which was programmed to use Martin B-26 Marauders. Once up to strength, this wing was programmed for assignment to the Eighth Air Force then being formed in Great Britain.

By now a major general, Doolittle and Maj. Gen. George E. Patton, Jr., left for General Eisenhower's London headquarters on August 5, 1942. The two met with General Eisenhower shortly thereafter and, according to Doolittle, "Ike took an immediate dislike to me."

Despite this unfortunate clash of personalities, Jimmy Doolittle kept working at fitting himself and his units into the upcoming Eighth Air Force. It wasn't easy. Aware of the fact that his boss disliked him made it difficult. But he continued to do his best, struggling to improve his organization, despite the verbal flak directed his way. At last, the Eighth Air Force was operationally ready.

During August 1942, it launched its first bombing mission. Eighteen Flying Fortresses (B-17s) flew against a freight railroad yard in France. In December 1942, fifty-three B-17s made their first attack on the German homeland.

During this time, Major General Doolittle was also responsible for helping to organize the Fifteenth Air Force. Using elements of the North African Air Force as a nucleus, the Fifteenth Air Force was organized on November 1, 1943. From its inception, Doolittle was in command. However, he received orders to take command of the Eighth Air Force in January 1944. This new command consisted of three bombardment divisions, a fighter command, and a

[32]

A B-17 "Flying Fortress"

service command. The Eighth Air Force then commenced strategic attacks on German industry. They bombed factories and submarine pens, gave fire support to ground troops, and raided V-weapon launch sites used to target on London. During that year, Jimmy Doolittle received his third star, thus becoming a lieutenant general.

Following the defeat of Germany, Doolittle and the Eighth Air Force headed for the Pacific area. They helped bomb what remained of Japanese forces. On August 6, 1945, the first atomic bomb was dropped on Hiroshima. On August 14, 1945, Japan surrendered, and on September 2, Japan signed a formal capitulation.

Now was the time for Jimmy Doolittle to return to civilian life. Air Force personnel called him in and explained how much money he would receive in retirement pay as a three-star general on active combat duty. He refused to accept any such money. To satisfy income tax requirements, he had all of his retirement pay divided and sent to the Air Academy Foundation and the Air Force Aid Society.

Lt. Gen. Jimmy Doolittle, the boy who was forever in trouble, and not too good at studies and classroom behavior, returned to civilian life. He worked his way up to become director of a large oil company and consultant director in several corporations.

In mid-June 1985, President Reagan pinned a fourth star on Jimmy Doolittle. A fitting conclusion to a great military flier's career.

Lt. Gen. Jimmy Doolittle

Place of birth: Columbus, Ohio.

Date of birth: November 15, 1906.

Education: Ohio State University.

Married: Helen Maitland, 1934.

Characteristics: Hardworking, persistent, innovative, courageous, had ability to lead men, a natural-born teacher of tactics.

Major commands and accomplishments:

1928 commissioned second lieutenant in ROTC.

1929 assigned to the Twenty-seventh Pursuit Squadron.

1940 took command of squadron of Thirty-fourth Bomb Group.

1942 given command of 305th Bombardment Group.

1943 as a colonel, named commander of Third Bombardment Division.

1944 promoted to major general and given command of Twentieth Bomber Command.

1945 commanded Twenty-first Bomber Command in Guam.

1947 now a lieutenant general, assumed command of U.S. Air Forces in Europe.

1951 became youngest four-star general since Ulysses S. Grant.

1961 appointed chief of staff, United States Air Force.

CURTIS E. LeMAY

A couple of young people from the farmlands of Ohio got married on November 25, 1905. They promptly moved to the nearest big city. The young fellow's name was Erving LeMay and the girl's name was Arizona Carpenter. Railroading was big in those days, and Erving managed to get a job as a structural ironworker with one of the lines. Unfortunately, the job did not last long. So the young couple moved.

The husband found another job. This time it was as a carpenter in Columbus. But that job also came to an abrupt end. Erving found another job, they moved; he lost that job and they moved again. At one time or another, Erving was employed as a construction worker, handyman, gardener, carpenter, and a perpetual seeker of better employment. It was as though he was chasing a rainbow.

Moving became a way of life. The LeMays were occupational nomads. On November 15, 1906, the first of three sons and two daughters was born to Erving and Arizona LeMay. He was named Curtis. Almost as if to celebrate the event, the family moved. In fact, one of the earliest memories of Curtis E. LeMay is of moving. These job shifts weren't limited to state boundaries either. The

[37]

ever-expanding LeMay troop set up housekeeping in Pennsylvania, Montana, and as far west as California.

As a young child, Curtis developed wanderlust. It was as if he had an inbred urge to see who lived down the street and around the corner. At first, one of the neighbors would come across the toddler playing some distance away. They'd bring him home. As time went on, the distances increased. Frequently, the police had to be called upon to help find the wanderer. When this happened, Curtis usually got a whipping from his father. The punishment didn't seem to be a deterrent, for in a day or two, he would disappear again.

Somewhere in his boyish consciousness, World War I came and went. He remembers November 11, 1918, for that was the day peace was declared. There were parades and crowds cheering and flags being waved and uniformed figures strutting about.

After that there were combat fliers going around the country staging aerial acrobatics in surplus warplanes. These daring young men performed loops and wingovers, with some even taking a man aloft who would leap out of the speeding plane and parachute to earth. These fliers and their flying machines never failed to attract a crowd. They would even take onlookers aloft at the going rate of a dollar a minute.

There were no such things in those days as flying restrictions or mechanical regulations. If the engine turned the propeller, hopefully, the plane usually went up. If the engine quit in flight, the plane came down in the nearest open space. Should it then be necessary to take off from some farmer's field, all that was needed was a woman's silk stocking flying from a stick to indicate the direction and force of the wind.

It took guts to fly, and young Curt LeMay admired these gypsy airmen. He wanted to ride with them. This, however, required money. To earn that money LeMay took on a newspaper route. His efforts were just becoming fruitful when the family moved to Pennsylvania. This stay wasn't to last long, for the next year, 1919, the LeMay family was back in Ohio. Young Curt picked up another paper route and again began to save money. By the time he reached high school, he had worked up to being a newspaper distributor. Instead of handling just one newspaper route, he now had a group of boys working for him. Such self-employment kept him busy and was a heavy responsibility. Curt LeMay had to get his newspapers out every day—rain, snow, or sunshine. It was necessary to see that each route was covered, that his workers were dependable, and that his customers were satisfied. He learned the management of human resources and money this way.

At an early age Curtis LeMay became self-supporting. He had a busy life. He studied when he could spare the time and dreamed of the day he would be able to fly an airplane. The young man could not allocate time for sports and extracurricular activities. He had to save money and prepare himself for a better education. He did allow himself one diversion: the Boy Scouts.

In America, scouting was an adjunct to becoming a man. He liked hiking, camping, cooking over an open fire and—best of all—learning marksmanship. He became a good shot. To this day, Curt LeMay has the first rifle his father gave him for hunting: a lever-action Winchester .30 caliber.

Curt graduated from high school in Columbus, Ohio, in 1924 and had hopes of going to college. But work was the thing that occupied his consciousness. By now he had several jobs, and worked and saved during summer vacations.

One day he and a friend pooled five dollars to take an airplane ride with a barnstormer who owned a three-seater biplane. The gypsy pilot cranked up the old plane, took off, circled the unplowed field, and landed. That was it. Although the flight was short, Curt LeMay was hooked on flying.

In the fall of 1924, he enrolled as an engineering student at Ohio State University. Since his parents had again moved, he joined Theta Tau, an engineering fraternity, and lived at the fraternity house. As was expected of him, he joined the ROTC (Reserve Officer Training Corps). There was an antimilitary clique on campus voicing its desire to ban all future wars. A fine theory, LeMay thought, if other nations would respect the same pacifist views. Unfortunately, as he was to find out in later years, not all countries possessed such nonbelligerent attitudes.

Curt LeMay enjoyed the ROTC program and believed in its value. Additionally, ROTC enabled him to get in a little marksmanship. However, both shooting and fraternity social activities were limited for Curt LeMay. He had a job after school hours that required him to work half the night. During summer vacations he held down several jobs at the same time.

It was while Curt was in college that Charles Lindbergh flew across the Atlantic Ocean. The news media, as well as the general public, became aware of civilian aviation. Newspapers and magazines carried numerous pictures and a good deal of copy pertaining to flying. Radio broadcasters also devoted more airtime to the subject.

All this material was of interest to LeMay. He had experienced the thrill of flying. Now this publicity began to solidify his determination to become a pilot. To him this meant having to become an active part of the military, for they were the ones who had the best planes and teaching facilities.

Being an honor ROTC graduate helped LeMay. He received a reserve officer commission on June 14, 1928. With that commission he was able to join the Ohio National Guard as a second lieutenant, artillery. This allowed him to put in an application for the Army's new Air Cadet Program. After many trials and tribulations, LeMay finally got orders to report to March Field, California. The Army paid his cost of transportation. LeMay then became part of the November 1928 class, which had over one hundred members, a great many of whom were later to die in the war.

In those times it was thirty days as a basic student (disparagingly called "dodos"), plus four months as a cadet. Dodos were housed in winterized tents; cadets in barracks. The first thirty days were devoted to physical training, which meant no flying.

The ROTC rifle team, Ohio State University, 1928.
Curtis LeMay is second from the right.

There was a good deal of harassment by upperclassmen and endless inspections. Beds had to be made in the military way, extra shoes properly aligned, and shirts hung just so. It was trial by torment. A number of applicants couldn't, or wouldn't, take the constant irritation. They quit the program.

For those who persisted, such as LeMay, there was the basic training. In LeMay's case basic flying proved to be a struggle because of inadequate instructions. It became an almost do-it-yourself course in flying. Things were tough. Many cadets were dropped from the program. The remnants of the class finally reached Kelly Field, just outside of San Antonio, Texas. Here at last LeMay was able to do a little real flying in what were considered fast planes. Finally, he won his wings, as part of the Air Corps Advanced Flying School, class of October 1929.

LeMay's first assignment was to Selfridge Field, Michigan. It was there he became active with the CCC (Civilian Conservation Corps), a volunteer group of workers, and was also assigned as a pilot to fly in the government's experiment in transporting mail by airplane.

While on duty at Selfridge Field, LeMay met Helen Maitland, a young woman from Cleveland, Ohio, who was doing postgraduate work in dental hygienics at Michigan University. They were married in 1934. Four years later, Patricia Jane, their only child, was born.

During these early days of his career, LeMay had some good luck, some bad. His skills, however, were superior.

By 1936, First Lieutenant LeMay was the operations officer of the Forty-ninth Squadron, Second Bomb Group. This group had been formed in France during World War I under the title of First Day Bombardment Group. It was reconstituted in 1924 and trained with B-17s. It was engaged in testing flying equipment, developing new air tactics, and flying mercy missions.

On September 1, 1939, Germany invaded Poland. War was declared on Germany. By then LeMay was a major in the U.S. Army Flying Service.

Having become chief of staff, General George C. Marshall approved of a survey flight to Cairo by a B-24 bomber. Curt LeMay was named copilot. The plane took off from Washington, D.C., and headed for Africa via Brazil. The flight over and back was successful. In all, it covered 26,000 miles (41,600 km) without incident.

On Sunday morning, December 7, 1941, at 7:55 A.M., the Japanese attacked Pearl Harbor. America was at war. Curtis LeMay, originally trained as a pursuit pilot, had been transferred to bombers because of his navigational skills. On that fateful morning, he was operations officer of the Thirty-fourth Bomb Group, based at Westover Field, Massachusetts. Even before the smoke had cleared over Hawaii, Curt LeMay was on the move. Americans on the West Coast feared a Japanese invasion. The Thirty-fourth Bomb Group then became part of a defense force based at Pendleton Field, Oregon.

LeMay didn't stay with them long. As a colonel he trained and commanded the newly activated 305th Bombardment Group. That unit, and its B-17s, were moved to England to become part of the Eighth Air Force. The unit attacked such targets as submarine pens, harbors, shipyards, motor works, and marshalling yards in France, Germany, and the low countries. It was this unit, as part of the Eighth Air Force, that later bombed the navy yards at Wilhelmshaven, Germany.

In September 1943, the Third Bombardment Division was activated in England, and Curtis LeMay, now a brigadier general, took command. Known as a keen tactician, he led one of the greatest air missions of the European war. One hundred and forty-six B-17s attacked the Messerschmitt factory at Regensburg, Germany, while another 230 Flying Fortresses hit the vital ball-bearing factories.

Although American casualties were heavy (numerous B-17s were downed and hundreds of airmen lost), the effectiveness of this raid proved LeMay's contention that the most effective bombing was through maintaining a defensive formation and flying a

Curtis LeMay (center) in Europe prior to flying a mission

straight-in bomb run. The effects on German war production were devastating. The Nazis never recovered from the blow.

On May 8, 1945, Germany surrendered. By then Curt LeMay was a major general and placed in command of the Twenty-first Bomber Command. The Twenty-first had been created in Kansas during March 1944 and sent to Guam for the purpose of hitting Japan. It was so new it didn't have—and never developed—a unit insignia. It was moved to the Marianas late in 1944, assigned to the Twentieth Air Force, and given the task of very long range bombardment.

Curtis LeMay studied the situation and came up with a bombing technique that was to prove itself different and effective. Using B-29s, in which he flew missions, the Twenty-first blasted such heavily industrialized areas as Anshan, Manchuria. Because the B-29s had not been overly effective in high altitude forays against the Japanese, LeMay stripped his bombers of much of their defensive armament. These planes were then used for low-level night attacks carrying firebombs. As LeMay foresaw, Japanese cities were especially vulnerable to fire. Enemy defenses could not cope with these attacks.

The B-29 was the largest aircraft to be used in World War II combat. It had a wingspread of 141 feet (42 m) and was 99 feet (30 m) in length. It flew almost 35,000 missions and dropped about 170,000 tons of bombs on the enemy. Almost 420 B-29s were lost, but their gunners were credited with destroying over 1,300 Japanese aircraft.

It was a B-29 from the Twenty-first that dropped the first atomic bomb on August 6, 1945, and the second atomic bomb on August 9, 1945. On August 14, 1945, Japan surrendered.

Following the signing of formal surrender agreements on the deck of the U.S.S. *Missouri* in Tokyo Bay, Lieutenant General LeMay initiated an active research and development (R&D) program within the U.S. Air Force. On October 1, 1947, he assumed command of the U.S. Air Forces in Europe.

The following spring, Soviet authorities laid a blockade on all

land and river thoroughfares leading into Berlin. Lieutenant General LeMay set about supplying military and civilian needs through a massive "Berlin Airlift." He was successful in this effort. After one year and a few months, the Soviets lifted their blockade. The airlift operation was ended during September 1949. It was one of the greatest achievements in the history of aviation. The United States had carried 4,446,000,000 pounds of food into the beleaguered city of Berlin.

When the Korean War broke out in June 1950, LeMay was head of the Strategic Air Command (SAC), and incorporated the first jet bombers into his command. In 1951, LeMay was promoted to four-star general. He thus became the youngest four-star general since Ulysses S. Grant.

Following nine years as SAC commander, Curtis LeMay was named vice–chief of staff. Shortly after taking over this job, he flew a KC-135 jet down to Buenos Aires to hand deliver a letter from President Eisenhower to President Aramburu. This was accomplished during Argentina's Aviation Week and was basically a goodwill flight. However, it covered 6,322.85 miles (10,116.56 km) without refueling; elapsed time was thirteen hours, two minutes, fifty-one seconds. The endeavor established a distance record for an unrefueled, nonstop jet aircraft.

Curtis E. LeMay was named chief of staff in 1961. On February 1, 1965, he retired from the Air Force. However, like so many great Americans, the termination of his military career did not spell the end of his usefulness. On leaving the Air Force, LeMay took over as an executive with a large industrial firm. Later, he became the vice-presidential running mate for Governor George Wallace when he made an unsuccessful bid for the presidency of the United States.

Gen. Curtis E. LeMay

Place of birth: Brooklyn, New York.

Date of birth: September 15, 1906.

Date of death: December 26, 1971.

Education: West Point, class of 1928.

Married: Lorraine Muller, December 29, 1930.

Nickname: Rosy.

Characteristics: Industrious, diligent, athletic, loyal, patriotic, fearless, argumentative.

Major commands and accomplishmnents:

1930 assigned to First Pursuit Group.

1942 operations officer, Far East Air Force, Java.

1944 commanding general, Seventy-third Bomb Wing (H), Saipan.

1946 director of information, Army Air Force headquarters.

1948 became commander of Fifteenth Air Force.

1959 commander in chief, Pacific Air Forces, Hawaii.

1963 retired from military and became president of USO (United Service Organizations).

EMMETT O'DONNELL, JR.

Brooklyn, New York, was a family place in 1906. Row houses, paved streets, horses and buggies, kids playing stickball in vacant lots, and police walking beats on which little or nothing occurred. The city subway was still new, and there was talk of constructing a bigger and better bridge across the East River—traffic was just too heavy for the old Brooklyn Bridge.

It seemed as if the borough of Brooklyn had everything. At least that was what a recently married couple named O'Donnell thought when they chose to settle there. On September 15, 1906, a healthy baby boy was born to the pair. He was given the name of Emmett O'Donnell, Jr.

The newborn child developed a hearty appetite. He expanded just as Brooklyn itself did. The borough went from being one of the smallest in New York City to becoming one of the largest. Emmett, Jr., kept pace with the area's growth. He sprouted from babyhood to boyhood. Then came school, books, and the drudgery of homework. Emmett, Jr., was not the best student. He excelled in sports, studied a little, passed most of his tests, and flunked a few. But he kept at it.

Then there was high school and girls and dances. It was at this period in his life that Emmett, Jr., began to show initiative. He

[49]

became president of the Scholastic Society and the student body. While in high school, he also voiced a secret thought he'd been nurturing for some time. He wanted to go to West Point Military Academy.

Acting on this ambition, he went to see Congressman William E. Cleary, who nominated him for an appointment. All of this took Emmett, Jr.'s, family by surprise. They had expected him to enter college in preparation for a career in medicine.

Finally, in the spring of 1924, Emmett, Jr., graduated from Brooklyn Manual Training School. One year later, he entered West Point Military Academy in New York State. It was there he earned the nickname Rosy, for his healthy complexion and tendency to blush. Despite this, the name Rosy O'Donnell became notable on the football field. It was as halfback that he teamed up with several all-American athletes of the period.

In June 1928, Emmett, Jr., graduated from the Point and was commissioned a second lieutenant, infantry. At about this time, the twenty-fifth anniversary of airplane flight was celebrated in Washington, D.C., and Amelia Earhart became the first woman to fly across the Atlantic. Aviation was making big headlines. In the fall of that year, Rosy entered flying training at Brooks Field, Texas.

Flying in open-cockpit airplanes was hot, dusty work, but Emmett O'Donnell, Jr., stuck with it, and in March 1930, he graduated from Advanced Flying School, Kelly Field, Texas. He was now a fully qualified aviator. His first decision was to marry a young woman he'd been courting for some time. Her name was Lorraine Muller and the ceremony was performed in December.

O'Donnell's initial assignment was to the First Pursuit Group at Selfridge Field, Michigan. During that period, the U.S. Postal Service was experimenting with flying the mail. The Army Flying Service had been called upon to assist in this undertaking. Venturesome young pilots were needed to make this endeavor a success. Rosy O'Donnell was the perfect choice. As a consequence, his duties included flying the mail from city to city. Ever the athlete, he also served as assistant football coach at West Point from 1934 through 1938. To accomplish this, he commuted between Michigan and New York.

"A change of orders," he announced to his wife one day in 1936.

"Where to?" she asked, with hope in her heart that it wasn't some outlandish post in a remote part of the country.

"Mitchell Field, New York," he announced. "To the Eighteenth Reconnaissance Group."

O'Donnell reported to his new post in December 1936. Not one to let grass grow underfoot, Rosy secured temporary orders that allowed him to attend the Air Corps Tactical School at Maxwell Field, Alabama. He graduated from the course in 1939. These were uneasy years in Europe. The Germans had reoccupied the Rhineland and Italy annexed Ethiopia by conquest. To cap such events, on August 23, 1939, the Soviet Union and Hitler's burgeoning Nazi government formed a nonaggression pact promising they would take no hostile acts against one another.

The military has always been a restless vocation. Rosy O'Donnell typified a man's life in the armed forces: not much pay, but a lot of travel. So when he again rushed home one day to proclaim, "I've been given a change of station," it came as no surprise to Lorraine.

"Where to this time?" she asked resignedly.

"Hawaii," Rosy declared. Her husband was a captain by then and had hopes of a command. His wishes were fulfilled: he would be squadron commander in the Eleventh Bombardment Group at Hickam Field on the island of Oahu.

The Eleventh Bombardment Group was to play a big part in Rosy O'Donnell's career. It had originally been established in 1933 as the Eleventh Observation Group. During 1938 it was redesignated the Eleventh Bombardment Group (Medium). In Hawaii, during February 1940, it was both activated and redesignated the Eleventh Bombardment Group (Heavy). It trained in B-18s, but later received B-17s for operational purposes.

There was an almost complete lack of bombers in the Far East. As a consequence, the Army Air Forces decided to fly a squadron of bombers to the Philippines as soon as possible. On September 5, 1941, the Fourteenth Bombardment Squadron, made up of nine B-17s and seventy-five crewmen, under the command of recently promoted Maj. Rosy O'Donnell, left Hickam Field, Hawaii, and headed for its first scheduled stop at Midway Island, almost 1,200 miles (1,920 km) away.

At Midway, crewmen and officers worked around the clock to prepare themselves for the next leg of the journey. Many of those assigned to an aircraft slept on the ground within sight of their bombers. By 4:45 A.M. the following morning, all were again airborne. They flew 1,035 miles (1,656 km), where they landed at Wake Island at about 11:30 A.M.

In view of the fact that Rosy O'Donnell's next programmed stop, Port Moresby, New Guinea, required his bombers to pass over Japanese-held territory, from which country they wished to keep the flight a secret, he elected to take off at midnight. Flying at an altitude of 26,000 feet (7,800 m), the bombers flew blind, in a heavy rainstorm, without communications, and managed to hold formation until they covered the 2,200-mile (3,520-km) trip.

Although welcomed by Port Moresby officials, and given every assistance, O'Donnell's destination was Clark Field, the Philippines. To this end, his squadron pushed on to Darwin, Australia, almost 1,000 miles (1,600 km) away. They covered the distance in six and a half hours.

Early in the morning on September 12, Rosy O'Donnell led his squadron on the final leg of their journey. En route, the bombers

As a young pilot, O'Donnell flew the mail from city to city for the U. S. Postal Service.

ran into bad weather. Major O'Donnell immediately ordered them into an echelon (steplike arrangement) that kept them from 100 to 400 feet (30 to 120 m) above the water. The bombers reached Clark Field in the Philippines in the late afternoon during a rainstorm.

Emmett O'Donnell, Jr., had led his forces in what has now become recognized as a historic flight—a flight made so difficult because of misleading weather reports, poor maintenance facilities, and lack of proper refueling equipment. It is interesting to note that the maximum flying distance of a B-17 is listed as only 2,100 (3,360 km) miles.

Unfortunately, the very people the United States was striving to impress the most were impressed the least. For even as this epic flight was underway, Admiral Yamamoto, commander in chief of Japan's Combined Fleet, was having his staff perfect plans for an attack on Pearl Harbor. Japanese planes were launched against the United States fleet at 6:00 A.M., December 7, 1941. Their target lay at rest 275 miles (440 km) to the south. Maj. Rosy O'Donnell was still in the Philippines when word reached him that Pearl Harbor was under attack. Before he or anyone else could react to the news, the Japanese Fourteenth Army struck at the Philippines with both air and land forces. The devastation they inflicted was overwhelming. More than half of Gen. Douglas MacArthur's air force was destroyed on the ground. MacArthur was Commander, U.S. Armed Forces, Far East.

"Counterattack! Strike back!" That was Rosy O'Donnell's reaction.

A wave of enemy planes roared in on Clark Field, Manila. This forced the remaining American bombers to take to the air or be destroyed on the ground. Rosy O'Donnell got one B-17 airborne. He then selected as his target a Japanese heavy cruiser, plus its destroyer escort.

Once over the enemy fleet, O'Donnell ordered his bombs to be dropped. "Can't," the bombardier replied. "The bomb releases won't work."

"Fix 'em," Rosy called over the intercom. "We'll make another run over the target."

By now the Japanese cruiser was fully alert. Its antiaircraft defenses were in all-out operation. They set up a wall of gunfire. O'Donnell flew through the flak. The bomb releases still refused to operate.

"We'll go in again," Rosy said.

"What about enemy planes?" a voice shrieked over the intercom. "They're closing in."

"So are we," Rosy snapped as he swung the bomber toward its target.

It took five runs over the target before all the bombs were off-loaded. For such heroic persistency, Maj. Rosy O'Donnell was awarded the Distinguished Flying Cross.

Then came the horrible task of withdrawing before enemy ground forces. Rosy O'Donnell's group fought in the air whenever they could and with the infantry when not airborne. Slowly, American forces had to withdraw to Mindanao, another island in the Philippines. Rosy O'Donnell and six hundred men of the Nineteenth Bombardment Group were loaded aboard an inter-island freighter. Their instructions were to repair and improve airfields near the Del Monte pineapple plantation.

As a major in the Air Corps, O'Donnell was bitter over what had happened at Clark Field. Both the landing strip and the B-17 bombers based there had proven inadequate to do battle. Clark Field was little more than a grass plot, on which were a few ramshackle hangars. The B-17 bomber had no tail gun and was therefore helpless against an attack from the rear.

As the inter-island steamer headed south, it was spotted by a four-engine Japanese seaplane. The enemy aircraft circled and came in for a bomb drop. All was confusion aboard the ship.

"We had no antiaircraft guns with which to fight back," Rosy was to recall later. "Some of my men had sidearms. They took to shooting at the swooping bomber. But a handgun isn't likely to do much damage against a fast-moving aircraft."

*Rosy O'Donnell (left) inspects an
aerial chart before flying a mission.*

The plane had plenty of time, but its marksmanship was poor. It made a bomb run—and missed. It tried another and that missed, too. It swung around for a third try. Rosy raced for the ship's wheelhouse.

"Do something," he yelled at the skipper. "Make it look like we've been hit."

The master of the freighter poured out a thick cloud of black smoke and dumped a spill of oil overboard. The impression given was that the vessel was severely wounded and on fire. The sea-plane left the scene, confident it had sunk an Allied ship.

It was during this Philippine fighting that a B-18 bomber had been found in an isolated spot of jungle.

"Let's take a look," Rosy said. "Perhaps it can be salvaged."

"No way," one investigator told him. "It's overgrown with jungle vines and the tires are suffering from dry rot."

"Let's give it a try," Rosy stubbornly insisted. "Let's take a team out there and see what we can do with the old bird."

The results proved amazing. A party of men, pushed to their greatest capabilities, and led by a competent officer, cut the B-18 bomber free. In addition, they dragged it onto an airstrip, refurbished its engines, and put the decrepit bird into flying condition. Rosy O'Donnell was delighted. Here was another bomber in his inventory. Not much of one, but a bomber, nevertheless. It had only three .30-caliber machine guns and two 850-horsepower engines that could push the heap along at a leisurely 200 miles (320 km) an hour.

It was then the ax fell.

"Rosy," a superior officer directed, "we have this official who must get to Australia. That old B-18 you refurbished should do the trick."

An order is an order. O'Donnell laid out a flight plan and managed to get the old bird into the air. His original intention was to land at a small island held by the Allies. Here he would refuel and depart as soon as possible.

"We'll never make it," Rosy confided to his copilot.

"Never make what, Rosy?"

"Never get the crate to fly again once we put her on the ground. She's just worn out in too many places."

"So what do we do, Rosy?"

"Keep going. We've got a tail wind. That might help blow us to Australia."

This is just what happened. They made their destination and were informed of two things. First, the Japanese had previously occupied the island where they were scheduled to refuel. Second, there wasn't another five minutes of flying time left in the fuel tank.

The thought of what they had barely missed was appalling to the crew. They would either have had to ditch in shark-infested waters or been captured by the enemy. Either event would no doubt have been fatal.

On his return to the Philippines, Rosy O'Donnell and some of his group fell back to Java. This was the most populous island in the Netherlands East Indies (now called Indonesia). It was known to be a keystone for a Japanese invasion of Australia. Because of its strategic importance, the entire Japanese Sixteenth Army was thrown into an all-out attack. Allied defenders were exhausted, ill-equipped, and in no condition to put up resistance. The island fell into enemy hands.

From January 20, 1942, when Rosy O'Donnell arrived in Java, until the first of March, at which time the island was captured by the Japanese, he served as operations officer in the Far East Air Force. He was then evacuated to India, where he became assistant chief of staff for operations of the newly organized Tenth Air Force.

This was a difficult job. The Tenth Air Force had been formed at Patterson Field, Dayton, Ohio. It was a theoretical organization until assigned to India. There it pulled together whatever Allied bombers remained in the area and declared them to be the Tenth United States Air Force. On April 3, 1942, Rosy O'Donnell programmed these combat-weary planes into executing their first mission. This was a bombing run against the Andaman Islands, a group of islands in the Bay of Bengal.

In March 1943, Rosy O'Donnell, now a colonel, was ordered to Washington, D.C., to be chief of Gen. Henry (Hap) Arnold's advisory council. Typical of O'Donnell's form of fearlessness, he approached General Arnold and told him he wanted to fly one of the new B-29 bombers in combat.

"No," Arnold is reported to have said in a conclusive voice. "I need you here in Washington."

O'Donnell began to argue the matter. Hap Arnold, a strong-willed man with a temper, was sick of hearing about B-29 bombers and the problems they entailed. He told O'Donnell as much. O'Donnell persisted in arguing the matter. Finally, in a burst of anger, Arnold picked up a paperweight and threw it at Rosy. The paperweight clipped O'Donnell, who caught it on the rebound and tossed it back at his boss.

It was this type of persistency that got O'Donnell what he wanted. A few months later, in March 1944, O'Donnell was appointed commanding general of the Seventy-third Bomb Wing at Smoky Hill Army Air Field, Salina, Kansas.

Brig. Gen. Rosy O'Donnell diligently trained the Seventy-third Bomb Wing for six months, then led it to the island of Saipan. When the vanguard of the Seventy-third arrived in October 1944, they were flabbergasted at what they found. Landing strips were still under construction, housing was minimal, and the U.S. Marines were still battling the Japanese on parts of the island. However, a week after they first landed in force, the place was operational to a minor degree.

Additional ground troops of the Seventy-third arrived at Saipan by water on September 16, and the regular headquarters reached Saipan on October 12. The bombardment groups (497th, 498th, 499th, and 500th), plus supporting groups, continued arriving during October and November. Less than one month later, the Seventy-third Bomb Wing was ready to begin bombing Tokyo.

It was then Rosy O'Donnell sprang a surprise on the residents of Tokyo. On November 24, 1944, as the Japanese people were celebrating a two-day harvest festival, they suddenly looked to the skies. One hundred and eleven American bombers roared in to liven up the party.

The B-29 bombers approached Tokyo from two different directions and spewed a rain of bombs over the city. This was just two years, seven months, and six days after Jimmy Doolittle's flight from a place called Shangri-la.

At the controls of the lead bomber was Rosy O'Donnell; his copilot was Maj. Robert K. Morgan. "We can expect," he had warned his contingent on leaving Saipan, "to meet heavy enemy fighter resistance."

In truth, they met little. A mixed bag of Japanese fighters closed in on the Americans. Of those Japanese fighter aircraft daring to attack, B-29 gunners claimed seven kills, eighteen probables, and nine damaged.

"We'll do it again," Rosy O'Donnell assured his enthusiastic bomber pilots upon their return. On March 9, 1945, B-29 bombers of the Seventy-third Wing lifted off from Isley Field, Saipan, to join a larger force. Almost 350 American bombers had assembled to unload approximately 2,000 tons of firebombs on Tokyo, the world's third largest city.

The bombers turned the metropolis of wood, narrow streets, and inefficient firefighting equipment into a burning cauldron. Thirty minutes after the first bomb struck, flames were out of control. Two days later, the 16 square miles (42 sq km) hit by American bombers were still burning.

This action was retribution for the Japanese attack on Pearl Harbor. It was the beginning of the end. Japanese war leaders were helpless against a constant influx of American bombers. Nevertheless, belligerent Japanese military leaders refused to surrender. There was little America could do but resort to the use of atomic bombs. This carried an undeniable message: Surrender, or be blasted off the map.

Following the second nuclear bomb at Nagasaki, the emperor of Japan called an imperial conference and announced to his Army and Navy chiefs of staff that Japan must surrender. These warriors accepted the decision badly. They pointed out that Japan had over five hundred kamikaze pilots in training, plus a large army of die-hard fanatics remaining on the home islands. The emperor refused to listen.

On August 14, 1945, the emperor of Japan broadcast on the radio to his war-weary people that Japan was surrendering.

Tokyo Bay, Japan, was the scene for the formal signing of unconditional surrender documents. This took place aboard the battleship U.S.S. *Missouri* on September 2, 1945, as hundreds of B-29 bombers flew overhead.

Never one to lay back and wait, General O'Donnell made his presence felt soon after the war ended. He was appointed Steering and Coordinating Member of the Permanent Board of Defense and the joint Brazil-United States Defense Commission.

Now a major general, O'Donnell became commander of the Fifteenth Air Force at Colorado Springs, Colorado, in October 1948. He moved with the organization to March Air Force Base, California, on November 7, 1949.

General O'Donnell had much to be proud of in being named to head the Fifteenth Air Force. That organization had an outstanding combat record.

"We were activated during 1943 in the Mediterranean theater during World War II," he was quick to tell a newcomer. "The Fifteenth bombed targets in France, Italy, Czechoslovakia, Poland, Austria, Hungary, and the Balkans right up until German forces surrendered unconditionally."

When the Korean War broke out in 1950, General O'Donnell took a nucleus of the Fifteenth Air Force to the Far East. There he organized the Far East Bomber Command with headquarters in Japan. His first B-29 units to arrive in Japan accomplished the outstanding feat of carrying out a bombing mission against North Korea within thirty-six hours after arriving.

General O'Donnell, now a three-star lieutenant general, was recalled to the United States. He was named deputy chief of staff for personnel at Air Force headquarters, Washington, D.C. He remained in this position until August 1, 1959, at which time he was given his fourth star and named commander in chief, Pacific Air Forces, with headquarters at Hickam Air Force Base, Hawaii.

His retirement from the military in 1963 did not lessen General O'Donnell's desire to serve his country. Shortly thereafter, he became president of the United Service Organizations (USO), a voluntary nonprofit corporation.

The USO operates worldwide in more than 160 locations, including mobile port centers in the Mediterranean Sea and Pacific area. In the United States and overseas, the USO is closely interwoven with United States military troop strengths.

General Emmett O'Donnell, Jr., was still active in this position when he died on December 26, 1971.

Gen. Emmett O'Donnell, Jr.

Place of birth: Boyertown, Pennsylvania.

Date of birth: June 28, 1891.

Date of death: July 14, 1974.

Education: West Point, class of 1914.

Nickname: Tooey.

Characteristics: Imaginative, pugnacious, reliable, hard-working, resolute, a brilliant tactician.

Major commands and accomplishments:

1917 commanded Thirty-first Aero Squadron in World War I.

1918 flight leader 13th Squadron, Second Pursuit Group.

1920 became commander of Kelly Field, Texas.

1921 commanded First Pursuit Group, Selfridge Field, Mich.

1929 commanded Seventh Bombardment Group. During this time set refueling endurance flight with Army plane *Question Mark.*

1933 became Chief of Training and Operations, Office of Chief of Air Corps.

1942 given command of Eighth Air Force.

1943 commanded the Northwest African Air Force.

1945 commanded U.S. Strategic Air Forces, Guam.

1946 nominated commander of the Army Air Forces.

1947 appointed first chief of staff, United States Air Force.

CARL
SPAATZ

Carl Spaatz was born on June 28, 1891, into a Pennsylvania Dutch family living at 31 S. Reading Avenue in Boyertown. He was one of five children. Originally, his last name was spelled Spatz, with one *a*. However, people mispronounced the name so often, to sound like spats, a man's ankle covering, a second *a* was added to give it more of an "ah" sound.

For an active boy like Carl Spaatz, there were advantages to having been born in Boyertown. It was a young community, populated by German-Americans, a majority of whom could trace their lineage in this country back before the American Revolution. Outdoor activities were plentiful. Hunting, fishing, camping, and sports were popular among the students of the one-room schoolhouse where Carl first learned to read and write.

There was an intangible quality about Boyertown. The Pennsylvania Dutch (who were Germans seeking to escape religious persecution in Europe) believed in the solidity of family life, relied upon hard work, practiced frugality, and were religious. These principles were instilled in the population. It was their way of life.

Carl's father, a printer by trade, who later became a state senator, was a firm believer in the teachings of Socrates. That ancient

[65]

Greek philosopher, who lived between 469 and 399 B.C., nurtured the belief that "a rightly trained mind would turn toward virtue." As a consequence, Carl's father saw to it that his children were reared in the patriotic schools of the district, whose teachers were well-grounded in the persuasion that if you spare the rod, you spoil the child.

Young Spaatz was a somewhat shy and modest youngster. Nevertheless, he was proficient in athletics. He was especially skillful at basketball, which had been invented the same year Spaatz was born, but blossomed rapidly throughout the United States. He was an average student in the lower grades, but his marks improved as he matured.

During his high school days, Carl found himself full of uncertainties about almost everything in life. He seemed to live from one emotional crisis to another. What did he want to be in life? Who would he take to the next school dance? Why did he always have to cut the lawn and wash the family car?

He graduated from Boyertown High School in 1906. It was at this time that his doubts began to evaporate. He started to make hard-and-fast decisions about his own well-being. He elected to be a military man. That seemed to offer an interesting career. By the time he finished his education, he had managed to get himself an appointment to the U.S. Military Academy at West Point, New York. That was in 1910. He was promptly dubbed "Tooey," because of a resemblance to an upperclassman.

"A great period in my life," he was often heard to say in later years.

Cadet Carl Spaatz was a good student. He studied hard, was attentive to the rigors of military life, and showed a necessary amount of ingenuity. It was difficult, but he made it. On June 12, 1914, he graduated from West Point and was commissioned a second lieutenant of infantry. There was a great deal of discussion among classmates about who got what orders and where they were being sent. Spaatz was ordered to the Twenty-fifth Infantry at Schofield Barracks, Hawaii.

It was a fine assignment, the cream of the crop. However, Lieutenant Spaatz was not content with the drudgery of garrison life. He applied for aviation training. On October 13, 1915, he was detailed as a student at the Aviation School, San Diego, California. Spaatz's career was off.

Border unrest had been brewing between Mexico and the United States. Abruptly, a Mexican revolutionary named Pancho Villa crossed into the United States and, on the night of March 8–9, 1916, raided the city of Columbus, New Mexico.

"A number of Americans have been killed and robbed," Gen. John J. Pershing received word from Washington. "You are ordered to pursue Villa into Mexico."

In keeping with these orders, General Pershing crossed the border in chase of the bandit. Shortly thereafter, Tooey Spaatz was assigned to the Mexican border as a member of the First Aero Squadron to assist in squashing this short-lived incident.

In the meantime, a European war had broken out between Germany (and its allies) and Great Britain (and its allies). As the conflict progressed, it became apparent that the United States was going to be drawn into what became World War I.

Spaatz went to France with the American Expeditionary Forces, in 1917, as commander of the Thirty-first Aero Squadron. Now a major, Spaatz was then given command of United States training at the old, famed Air Service School, Issoudun, France. It was while assigned to training duties that he took leave—some say he went AWOL—and flew with a British fighter unit. In one engagement, he shot down two German fighter planes in a single action. Later, he was credited with a third *Fokker* plane.

When questioned about his actions, Spaatz acknowledged, "At one time I narrowly missed being captured when my gas tank almost ran dry."

Although he was censured for this bit of extracurricular activity, Tooey Spaatz was awarded the Distinguished Service Cross. Such a decoration is awarded a person who, while serving in any capacity with the U.S. Armed Forces, distinguishes himself by

extraordinary heroism against an armed enemy of the United States.

Tooey Spaatz had certainly met these requirements.

By 1918, World War I had come to an end. American troops were returned to the States. The armed forces were reduced and shuttled about, and promotions were held to a minimum. Many good men felt that military life offered a poor future. Tooey Spaatz thought otherwise. He saw aviation as a way of life with a promising outlook. He elected to stay with the army and fly.

These were doldrum days for the military. Spaatz's pay was reduced, and he was dropped one rank (because of a reduction in the Armed Forces). He was assigned to a flying field in California and then transferred to Texas and once more promoted to major. It was a homeless sort of existence, but he was getting in some flying, which he loved.

His superior officer was a Col. Henry (Hap) Arnold, who was destined to become one of only four permanent five-star generals in the history of the United States. Yet at one period, when reductions were rampant, Tooey Spaatz found himself outranking his commander. To Spaatz, this was an impossible situation. As a remedy, and to save Hap Arnold embarrassment, Spaatz put in for an immediate transfer.

By 1920, as a major, Tooey Spaatz commanded Kelly Field in Texas, after which he did a stint in Washington.

There were big things happening in the world of flying. Charles Lindbergh flew the Atlantic, and civilians became aviation-conscious. Tooey Spaatz organized a team to refuel a plane while in flight. The object of the exercise was to see how many hours of continuous flying one plane could endure. A tri-motored Fokker was selected and named *Question Mark*. With Tooey Spaatz in command, and Capt. Ira C. Eaker and Capt. Elwood

Spaatz as a student at the Aviation
School in San Diego, California

[69]

"Pete" Quesada as crew members, the plane was kept aloft for a record-breaking 150 hours, 50 minutes, and 15 seconds. This was a continuous flight of over six days. During this experiment, the plane flew 11,000 miles (17,600 km) and was refueled forty-three times, nine of these being at night. For this feat, Tooey Spaatz was awarded the Distinguished Flying Cross.

After that, Major Spaatz was given command of the Seventh Bombardment Group based at Rockwell Field, California. He settled into the work of training, participating in aerial reviews, dropping food to marooned or lost people, and taking part in maneuvers and aerial experiments.

Following that, he was given command of the First Bombardment Wing, based at March Field, California, and in June 1933, he returned to Washington as chief of the Air Corps' Training and Operations Division. Then it was back to school again. He was assigned to the Command and General Staff school at Fort Leavenworth, Kansas. It was while at this school that Carl Spaatz was promoted to Lieutenant Colonel and as such graduated in June 1936. When he returned to Washington, he became assistant executive officer to the chief of the Air Corps. Suddenly, in 1939, the world was in a flurry. The Nazi army invaded Poland. Great Britain, France, Australia, and New Zealand were forced to declare war on Germany. In that same year, Carl Spaatz was promoted to colonel.

The Battle of Britain was well under way when Colonel Spaatz was sent to England as a special military observer. To accomplish this task in a thorough manner, he was frequently seen sitting on a rooftop with a pair of binoculars. In this way, he could watch the effectiveness of German bombs. It was on this subject that he came into conflict with Joseph Kennedy, America's ambassador to Great Britain. Kennedy viewed the bombings from a political standpoint.

"A German invasion of England is inevitable," Kennedy reported to Washington.

Tooey Spaatz's record-breaking in-flight refueling endeavor

*During World War II, Spaatz was sent to England as
a special military observer. He is in the middle.*

"No way," Spaatz reported, "can the Nazis attempt an invasion of England until they first defeat the Royal Air Force."

Tooey Spaatz's insistence on this point of view gained him attention. His predictions were proving more correct by the day. Without air supremacy—which they never secured—the Germans were stopped at the English Channel.

Because of his insight into the European situation, Tooey Spaatz was recalled to Washington, given his first star, and named chief of the air staff at AAF headquarters.

On December 7, 1941, the Japanese attacked Pearl Harbor. A few months later, Spaatz was given his second star and promoted to the rank of major general. Now he was ready for the big step up. In May 1942, he was given command of the newly activated Eighth Air Force. In this capacity, he went to the European theater of operations.

The first Eighth Air Force bombing took place in August 1942, when eighteen B-17 Flying Fortresses staged a raid on a railroad marshalling yard near Rouen, France. The beginning of the following year saw fifty-three B-17s mounting an initial attack on the hinterland of Germany. They raided a U-boat construction yard at Wilhelmshaven.

In a postwar confession, Admiral Karl Donitz, supreme commander of the German navy's U-boat arm, stated that "up until those air raids, Germany was producing twenty submarines a month. Following that initial air attack, production started to drop off."

General Spaatz's accomplishments earned him the Legion of Merit award. However, with promotions and decorations came increased responsibilities. Additional duties were laid on Tooey Spaatz. He was named commanding general of all U.S. Army air forces in the European theater.

Having displayed great leadership, Tooey Spaatz was named commanding general of the Twelfth Air Force in late 1942. The Twelfth had been active in the fighting against Nazi general Erwin Rommel's tank forces. Called the Desert Fox, Rommel was experiencing great successes against British ground forces in Africa. So successful had Rommel been that Hitler named him a field marshal, an officer of the highest rank, while Mussolini, who was so certain of success, laid plans for a victory parade into the city of Cairo, Egypt.

"When the Twelfth began operations in Africa," Spaatz was to say, "it had relatively few planes with which to work."

Spaatz combined the Twelfth with the Royal Air Force and built the composite into a massive flying force. He named this the Northwest African Air Forces. Fighter planes from this force then set about cutting Rommel's supply lines. Within a short time, they succeeded in destroying eighty German transport planes. The Anglo-American force became known as the "Spaatzwaffe."

With the downfall of Rommel's forces came another star for Tooey Spaatz. Now a lieutenant general, Tooey was named deputy commander of the Mediterranean Allied Forces. This force was a consolidation of the Mediterranean Air Command with the Northwest African Air Forces. MAAF, as it was referred to, was created at an Allied conference in Cairo. President Roosevelt, Prime Minister Churchill, and Generalissimo Chiang Kai-shek were the principal participants at the meeting.

General Tooey Spaatz returned to England in January 1944. He was given command of the U.S. Strategic Air Forces in Europe.

Tooey's technique was to have his air forces strike at key arteries and transportation systems. The Spaatz tactic was one of supply-starvation directed against Nazi tank and air forces. So effective were his procedures that he became a firm believer in a theory he often voiced. "Air power, if properly applied, would eliminate the necessity for an Allied invasion of Europe."

This contention is still a subject for debate between advocates of air power and adherents of ground forces.

Following the May 7, 1945, complete surrender of German forces, which took place at Allied headquarters (SHAEF), in Reims, France, by Germany's Gen. Alfred Jodl, Tooey Spaatz was given further orders. He was assigned to Air Force headquarters in Washington. Sometime later, he assumed command of the U.S. Strategic Air Forces in the Pacific. His headquarters were then on Guam.

With Gen. Curtis LeMay as his chief of staff, Spaatz was to guide the final months of the B-29 campaign against Japan, including the dropping of atomic bombs on Hiroshima and Nagasaki. He was present at the signing of the unconditional surrender by the enemy at Tokyo, as he had been at Reims and Berlin.

Combat experience convinced Spaatz that the Air Force could accomplish its mission only if it maintained a force of adequate size, strategically deployed, and in a constant state of readiness. He believed that the first priority should be given to a strong strategic air force, but he also spoke out for cooperation among air, ground, and sea forces.

To keep a powerful air force alive, Spaatz wanted a strong National Guard and Air Force Reserve to provide trained replacements in time of national emergency. To support the air force, Spaatz urged a well-balanced program of research and development, a readily expandable aeronautical industry, and a well-informed public.

In February 1946, General Spaatz replaced Gen. H. H. (Hap) Arnold as the commanding general of the Army Air Forces. Spaatz had worked closely with Arnold since 1918.

Although demobilization had not as yet been fully accomplished, Spaatz decided to anticipate an independent air force by grouping the combat forces under three functional commands:

1. Strategic Air
2. Tactical Air
3. Air Defense Commands

The remainder of the framework consisted of five supporting commands in the United States and five overseas. All followed the traditional pattern of theater air commands established in

World War II. Foremost among the overseas commands were the U.S. Air Forces in Europe and the Far East Air Forces. These accounted for most of the combat strength outside the United States.

Shortly after 1946, the Air Force entered the supersonic era that Spaatz had long sponsored and was even then working on plans for the B-52 intercontinental bomber. This bomber has been the mainstay of the U.S. Air Force for many a decade since.

During October 1946, General Spaatz returned to the United States, and the following year he was nominated to become commander of the Army Air Forces. In September 1947, president Truman appointed him the first chief of staff of the newly created United States Air Force.

General Spaatz retired from the service on June 30, 1948. Upon retirement, he became active with numerous committees having to do with national security. He became chairman of the board for the Air Force Association in 1950.

General Carl (Tooey) Spaatz died on July 14, 1974.

Gen. Carl Spaatz

OFFICER RANK DURING WORLD WAR II

Second Lieutenant   One gold bar

First Lieutenant   One silver bar

Captain   Two silver bars

Major   One gold leaf

Lieutenant Colonel   One silver leaf

Colonel   A silver eagle

Brigadier General   One silver star

Major General   Two silver stars

Lieutenant General   Three silver stars

General   Four silver stars

General of the Air Force   Five silver stars (in a circle)

U.S. AIR FORCE COMMAND STRUCTURE DURING WORLD WAR II

FLIGHT: a formation of aircraft, usually three or more

SQUADRON: a formation of aircraft, usually six or more

GROUP: usually eighteen or more planes, such as the First Fighter Group

WING: a flexible unit usually made up of about fifty aircraft, such as the Fourth Bombardment Wing

DIVISION: a designation for certain offices or functions in the Air Force such as Civilian Personnel Division and the Sixth Air Division

COMMAND: an Air Force unit that is usually a wing or larger, over which an officer exercises authority

AIR FORCE: numbered, or named, military forces, such as the Eighth Air Force and the Second Air Force

GLOSSARY OF WORLD WAR II AVIATION TERMS

Ace: an expert combat pilot credited with not less than five victories

Aeronaut: pilot of a balloon

AFROTC: Air Force Reserve Officers Training Corps

Air Corps: a branch of the Army during World War II

Airfield and airdrome: both are used for the takeoff and landing of aircraft

Airship: a dirigible

AWOL: absent without leave

B: when used in connection with an aircraft, it means "bomber," such as the B-26 and B-29

Bailout: leaving an aircraft by parachute

Bandit: enemy aircraft

Barnstorming: flying a plane from one airdrome to another for the purpose of taking civilians for a flight

Blanket: a smoke concentration laid down to prevent enemy observation

Box formation: formation in which planes fly in a boxlike configuration

C-47: a twin-engine transport plane designed to carry heavy cargo and troops

Caliber: the diameter of a bullet, or shell

Ceiling: the maximum height at which an aircraft can fly

Commander: the officer in charge

Cruising radius: the distance a plane can travel and return to its base nonstop

Daredevil: a stunt flier who takes unnecessary risks

Ditch: to set a landplane on water under emergency conditions

Dodo: a trainee pilot who has not yet soloed

Drop tank: a tank that can be dropped in flight; frequently used in napalm (see below) bombing

Element: any subdivision or part of a military organization

Escort: a plane assigned to fly as protection for another aircraft

Evasive action: abrupt changes in altitude or direction to avoid detection, or attack, by an enemy

Fatigue clothing: working clothing for military personnel

Firepower: capacity to deliver gunfire

Flame bomb and/or fire bomb: a bomb constructed to cause excessive heat and flame

Formation bombing and/or attack: action by aircraft while holding their formation

Frag: the use of fragmentation bombs

Goof-off: a person who manages to avoid work

Gooney bird: name given the C-47 twin-engine, transport aircraft

Gun blister: a protuberance on an airplane from which a gunner fires a gun

H hour: the time at which an attack is to take place

Heavy bomber: a plane having gross weight of over 250,000 pounds (113,500 kg)

Horsepower: a power equal to raising 33,000 pounds (14,982 kg) one foot (30 cm) in one minute against the pull of gravity

Hypoxia: oxygen deficiency in the blood inducive to pilot unconsciousness and ultimate crash of aircraft

Interceptor: a plane designed to meet and engage an enemy aircraft

Intruder: an unidentified aircraft

Jettison: to lighten an aircraft by throwing out anything movable, as well as dropping bombs, fuel, cargo, and armament

Jockey: slang expression for a pilot

Kamikaze pilot: Japanese pilot assigned to make a suicidal crash on a target

Lead crew: a specially trained aircrew that flies the lead aircraft on a bombing mission

Leaflet bomb: propaganda leaflets dropped over enemy territory in a container

Light bomber: a plane having a gross weight of over 100,000 pounds (45,400 kg)

Loadmaster: aircrew member who supervises loading of aircraft

Maneuver: a military move taken in anticipation of a following move in hopes of a gained advantage from the first move

Medium bomber: plane having a gross weight of between 100,000 and 250,000 pounds

Mobilize: to convert a country and its people to a wartime basis

Monoplane: an airplane having only one wing

Napalm: a mixture of aluminum soap, explosives, and gasoline used in bombs and flame throwers

Occupied territory: territory held by the enemy

Officer candidate: a person undergoing rigorous, short-term training to qualify for an officer's commission

Outmanevuer: to gain an advantage over an opponent

Panic Button: slang expression for use of an ejection seat, or some other emergency

Prop wash: slang expression meaning gossip or rumors; also, turbulent air driven backwards by a propeller

Pylon: a tower used in an air race to mark a turn

R.A.F.: Royal Air Force

Railhead: point along a railroad track where supplies are unloaded

Ration(s): an allowance of provisions for one person for one day

Regular commission: an officer in the regular, active-duty air force

Reserve Commission: an officer in a military service held in reserve

Robot bomb: winged missile such as those used by the Germans to bomb the city of London

Sacred cow: slang for a special plane reserved for the sole use of a high-ranking official

Scatter bomb: a bomb that scatters its effect over a broad area

Skip bombing: releasing one or more bombs so that they bounce off a surface to hit a target

Snap roll: an aerial maneuver

Soup: slang for foul weather, such as fog or rain

Sweep: an offensive mission by several planes over an area

Tactical unit: a unit activated to fight, strafe, rake ground objects with gunfire, lay mines, and drop bombs against an enemy

Taxi: to drive an aircraft across the ground, or water, except for takeoff or landing

Tower: short for control tower

War game: a simulated battle

Wingman: a pilot who flies to the side, or rear, of an element leader

Zero: to adjust gunsights for accuracy

TYPES OF AIRCRAFT

B-17 Boeing Aircraft. Monoplane with four engines and a speed of about 252 miles (403 km) per hour. Known as the Flying Fortress. Improved in armament and incorporated refinements as World War II progressed.

B-18 Douglas Bolo. Deep-bellied plane that could accommodate 6,500 pounds (2,951 kg) of bombs. Armament was three .30-caliber machine guns. Speed was about 200 miles (320 km) per hour.

B-24 Consolidated Aircraft. Intended to be an improvement over the B-17. Had greater range and bomb load. Used extensively in Pacific. Possessed twin stabilizers and four engines.

B-25 North American Mitchell. Conventional twin-engine, twin-tail, medium bomber with tricycle landing gear. Could carry 3,000 pounds (1,362 kg) of bombs. Speed varied from 275 to 315 miles (440 to 504 km) per hour according to model.

B-26 Twin engine bomber, called "invader," developed by Douglas Aircraft.

B-29 Most advanced bomber used in World War II. Called Boeing Superfortress, it could carry up to ten tons of bombs. Armed with eight .50-caliber machine guns. Had four 2,200-horsepower engines, giving it a speed of 365 miles (584 km) per

[87]

hour at 25,000 feet (7,500 m), with a maximum range of 5,830 miles (9,328 km).

Fokker Any plane designed by A.H.G. Fokker, or by companies established by Fokker. These planes were fabricated in Germany during WWI and later in the U.S. and the Netherlands.

P-40 Curtiss Aircraft. Used extensively by Claire Chennault in China. Later models gave it a service ceiling of 32,400 feet (9,720 m) with speeds of 352 miles (563 km) per hour.

BIBLIOGRAPHY

Coffey, Thomas M. *Hap: The Story of the U.S. Air Force and the Man Who Built It.* New York: Viking Press, 1982.

Dunn, William R. *Fighter Pilot: The First American Ace of World War II.* Lexington, KY: University of Kentucky Press, 1982.

Glines, Carroll V., Jr. *Doolittle's Tokyo Raiders.* Salem, NH: Ayer Co. Publishers, 1979.

———. *The Compact History of the U.S. Air Force.* Salem, NH: Ayer Co. Publishers, 1979.

Ienaga, Saburo. *The Pacific War, 1931–1945: A Critical Perspective on Japan's Role in World War II.* New York: Pantheon, 1979.

McCombs, Don, and Fred L. Worth. *World War II Superfacts.* New York: Warner Books, 1983.

Snyder, Louis L. *World War II*, Revised edition. New York: Franklin Watts, 1981.

Sweeney, James B. *Army Leaders of World War II.* New York: Franklin Watts, 1984.

INDEX

Africa, 74

Air Cadet Program, 40

Air Corps Advanced Flying
School, 42, 50

Air Corps Tactical School, 51

Aircraft, types of, 87

Air Force, U.S., 77, 81

Air Forces in Europe, U.S., 45,
77

Air Service School, France, 67

American Expeditionary
Forces, 67

American Volunteer Group
(AVG), 18, 21

Army Air Corps, 21

Army Air Forces, commanding
general of the, 75, 77

Army Flying Service, 42, 50

Arnold, H. H. (Hap), 59, 69,
75

Atomic bomb, 45, 60, 75

Aviation Section, Signal Reserve Corps, 17, 27

Aviation terms, 83–86

B-17 (Flying Fortress), 32, 33,
42–43, 51, 53–55, 73, 87

B-18, 51, 57, 87

B-24, 43, 87

B-25, 29–30, 87

B-26, 32, 87

B-29, 45, 59–61, 75, 87–88

B-52, 77

Bendix Trophy, 28

Berlin Airlift, 47

Blind flight, first, 28

Chennault, Claire L., 12–21
Chinese Air Force, 17–18
education, 14–16
peacetime military service,
17

Chennault *(continued)*
  retirement (1936), 17
  World War I, 16–17
  World War II, 21
Chennault Air Force Base, 21
Chiang Kai-shek, 17–18, 74
China, 17–18, 21
Churchill, Winston, 74
Civilian Conservation Corps
  (CCC), 42
Clark Field, Philippines, 53–55
Congressional Medal of Honor, 32
Curtiss JN-4, 27

Desert Fox. *See* Rommel, Erwin
Distinguished Flying Cross,
  55, 70
Distinguished Service Cross,
  67
Dixon, Cromwell, 26
Doolittle, James H., 22–35
  acrobatic flying, 28
  Congressional Medal of
    Honor, 32
  education, 25–26
  peacetime achievements,
    28–29
  retirement, 35
  World War I, 26–28
  World War II, 29–30, 32,
    35

Earhart, Amelia, 50

Eighteenth Reconnaissance
  Group, 51
Eighth Air Force, 32, 35, 43,
  73
Eisenhower, Dwight D., 32, 47
Eleventh Bombardment
  Group, 51

Far East Air Force, 58, 77
Far East Bomber Command,
  61
Fifteenth Air Force, 32, 61
First Aero Squadron, 67
First Bombardment Wing, 70
First Day Bombardment
  Group, 42
First Pursuit Group, 50
Flying Fortress. *See* B-17
Flying Tigers, 18
Fokker aircraft, 67, 69, 88
Forty-ninth Squadron, Second
  Bomb Group, 42
Fourteenth Bombardment
  Squadron, 53
Fourth Bombardment Wing,
  32

Germany, 32, 35, 42–43, 45,
  51, 67, 70, 73–74
Great Britain, 70, 73

Italy, 51

Japan, 17–18, 21, 29–30, 35,
  45, 54–55, 57–61, 75

Java, Indonesia, 58
Jenny (Curtiss JN-4), 27

KC-135, 47
Kennedy, Joseph, 70
Korean War, 47, 61

Legion of Merit, 73
LeMay, Curtis E., 36–47
    Berlin Airlift, 47
    education, 39–40, 42
    jet aircraft record, 47
    Korean War, 47
    retirement, 47
    World War II, 42–43, 45,
        75
Lindbergh, Charles, 40, 69

MacArthur, Douglas, 54
Marshall, George C., 43
Mediterranean Allied Forces
    (MAAF), 74
Midway Island, 53

National Air Races, 28
Nineteenth Bombardment
    Group, 55
Nineteenth Pursuit Squadron,
    17
Northwest Africa Air Forces,
    74

O'Donnell, Emmett, Jr., 48–63
    Distinguished Flying
        Cross, 55

O'Donnell (continued)
    education, 50
    retirement, 63
    World War II, 51, 53–55,
        57–61

P-40, 18, 88
Patton, George E., Jr., 32
Pearl Harbor, Hawaii, 54
Permanent Board of Defense,
    61
Pershing, John J., 67
Philippines, 53–55, 57
Port Moresby, New Guinea, 53
Postal Service, United States,
    50

Question Mark (airplane), 69

Reagan, Ronald, 35
Rommel, Erwin, 73–74
Roosevelt, Franklin D., 30, 74
ROTC (Reserve Officers Train-
    ing Corps), 39–40, 41
Royal Air Force, 74

SAC (Strategic Air Command),
    47
Saipan, Mariana Islands, 59
Schneider Trophy Race, 28
Seventy Bombardment Group,
    70
Seventy-third Bomb Wing, 59–
    60
Soviet Union, 45, 47, 51

Spaatz, Carl, 31, 64–77
    awards, 67, 70, 73
    education, 66
    plane refueling exercise,
        69–70
    post-World War II activi-
        ties, 75, 77
    retirement, 77
    World War I, 67, 69
    World War II, 70, 73–75
Spaatzwaffe, 74
Strategic Air Command (SAC),
    47
Strategic Air Forces in Europe,
    U.S., 74
Strategic Air Forces in the Pa-
    cific, U.S., 74
Stunt flying, 17, 28, 38

Tenth Air Force, 58
Third Bombardment Division,
    43
Thirty-first Aero Squadron, 67
Thirty-fourth Bomb Group, 43
Thomas Morse (aircraft), 27
Thompson Trophy Race, 29
305th Bombardment Group,
    43
"Three Men on a Flying Tra-
    peze," 17
Tokyo, Japan, 59–60
Training and Operations Divi-
    sion, Air Corps, 70
Transcontinental speed
    records, 28–29

Twelfth Air Force, 73–74
Twentieth Air Force, 45
Twenty-first Bomber Com-
    mand, 45

Union of Soviet Socialist Re-
    publics. See Soviet Union
United Service Organizations,
    63
United States Military Acade-
    my, 50–51, 66
USO, 63

Wake Island, 53
West Point. See United States
    Military Academy
World War I, 28
    Chennault, Claire L., 16–
        17
    Doolittle, James H., 26–28
    Spaatz, Carl, 67, 69
World War II
    Air Force command struc-
        ture, 81
    Chennault, Claire L., 21
    Doolittle, James, H., 29–
        30, 32, 35
    LeMay, Curtis E., 42–43,
        45
    O'Donnell, Emmett, Jr.,
        51, 53–55, 57–61
    officer rank, 79
    Spaatz, Carl, 70, 73–75

York, Edward J., 30

ABOUT
THE
AUTHOR

James B. Sweeney, a retired lieutenant colonel of the U.S. Air Force, has a long history of military service. As a combat reporter in World War II, he was awarded a Bronze Star, four Battle Stars, and several commendation medals.

Colonel Sweeney has written many books for young people. He is the author of *A Combat Reporter's Report* and *True Spy Stories*, both published by Franklin Watts.